ELAINE'S BOOK

Volume 7
The Callaloo Poetry Series

Charles H. Rowell, *Series Editor*

Jay Wright
ELAINE'S BOOK

University Press
of Virginia
Charlottesville

THE UNIVERSITY PRESS OF VIRGINIA
Copyright © 1986 by Jay Wright
First published 1988

Library of Congress Cataloging-in-Publication Data

Wright, Jay.
  Elaine's book / Jay Wright.
    p. cm.—(The Callaloo poetry series ; v. 7)
  ISBN 0-8139-1201-6 (pbk.) : $8.95
  I. Title. II. Series.
PS3573.R5364E4   1988
811'.54—dc19   88-14133
                                              CIP

"Zapata and the Egúngún Mask" first appeared in *Callaloo,* no. 19 (1983); "Guadalupe-Tonantzin," "Tlazoltéotl," and "Guadalajara" appeared in *Callaloo,* no. 26 (1986); and "Ann Street," "Passionflower," "Orchid," and "Dandelion" in *Callaloo,* no. 27 (1986). "Madrid" first appeared in *The Yale Review* 77, no. 2 (Winter 1988).

Printed in the United States of America

Contents

Veil, I *1*
Seals, I *2*
Seals, II *4*
Hathor *5*
The Origin of Mary in a Cathedral Choir *7*
Yemanjá *9*
Zapata and the Egúngún Mask *11*
Confrontation *27*
Guadalupe-Tonantzin *28*
Tlazoltéotl *37*
Confrontation *40*
The Lake in Central Park *41*
Confrontation *43*
Ann Street *44*
Cornelia Street *45*
Confrontation *46*
Confrontation *47*
Confrontation *48*
Guadalajara *49*
Lisboa *52*
Madrid *54*
Confrontation *57*
Confrontation *59*
Orchid *60*
Passionflower *62*
Dandelion *64*

Confrontation 65
Confrontation 66
Confrontation 67
The Anatomy of Resonance 68
Journey to the Place of Ghosts 74
Saltos 77
The Power of Reeds 79
Desire's Persistence 82

ELAINE'S BOOK

Veil, I

There is something about the blood in a sunset
that answers no questions;
the tarnished veil of a halo refers us
to a dream we never had;
and whatever wakes in us
when the unseen loon calls
offers no consolation.
Can I speak of the heart here,
when nothing speaks to it?
Can the night's brush uncover crystals of longing
that master moon hides and rocks in the beech?
Given such suspicion,
it is too early to submit to the darkness.
You must commit yourself to the light's weave,
the distant clarity of a promise you may have
                              misunderstood.
Go on;
the sunset's veronica'd blood
promises consonance.
You will learn the veil's appeal to the light in you.

Seals, I

> Por un instante están los nombres habitados.
>
> Octavio Paz, *Semillas Para Un Himno*

A river flowed out of Eden to water the garden.
What has the river found?
Onyx, gold, and a substance which has hidden
                            behind its name.
Your name does not arise in Gilgamesh;
only the mask appears,
sainted seal of a serpent's grove,
root of the Immovable Spot,
the assurance that you will always move.
But, then, waters divide to frame a world.
A star turns east to west
          to remind you of its dark side.

I imagine evening, when the man comes,
following his lion-bird,
keeper of the pail and upraised branch.
We can see the man's night face
and you, in his shadow.
Down below,
the serpents swim in stillness.
And in this moment, the sun
is only a seed of desire.
We must insist that bliss is knowledge
of the evening's rising and the tree's root
slowly given to its coffin in water.

So I have placed you at the head of sacred things,
and called our habitation night.
A darker woman leans, invisible, at your ear.
She bears another earthen, covered pot,
in which my memory of you is held.

Seals, II

Lady of the Beasts,
Mountain Mother
Spear Hand
Visible Planet
Have I named you?
Will I come to the architrave
to consecrate my lost powers?
I have been a faithful son of the abyss,
one who curdles when my drum calls.
My singing is coarse cloth on a desert floor.
Whatever fires I light burnish an old man's knees.
Goddess of the living,
I am not one you would choose to redeem.
I take the steps below you much too swiftly.
I cannot endure the clarity
               of knowing your other name.

Hathor

Moonless dawn.
The cold house crackles.
Outside, the leafless trees creak
and sigh in the wind's caress.
That moan and cold's ache comfort you.

There should be a young man
to hang at the foot of your bed,
knees snell with duty and complaisance.
We shall call this civilization:
the astral calendars touting heaven's law,
priests rising from the dust to tutor the city,
a young man cognizant of your virtue.

Veritably, the Sumerian has marked you,
a wild and pillared thing,
                grueled in marshes.
Coldness recalls how you mothered the world
and a golden falcon, bull of your house.
In the room's cave silence,
we hear the dead one tap the wall.
He must be held, head east,
on the warm side of this grave.
He sleeps among his swords and cutting tools,
razors and bronzes; his rawhide sandals
flicker beneath an ostrich fan.
A dream has covered his linen body with hide.
Bull's legs ferry him among his water pots.

This body belongs to you,
an eternal presence, whose only gift is fulfillment.
Dawn finds me here,
searching the purple bruise of your faithfulness.
Who but she can you be?
Who but the one who submits
and is quickened by fire,
or is buried, by faith, beneath the hide,
able only to affirm that spirit's loss?
I mark your presence here,
bereft of the love you have sheltered
by being forever taken.

The Origin of Mary
in a Cathedral Choir

> At the age of five Cecilia saw a meteor, and
> thereupon decided to be an astronomer. She
> remarked that she must begin quickly, in case
> there should be no research left when she
> grew up.

Beauty is splendor veritatis, a radiance of truth.
The fact of revelation the eye beholds can never lie.
Old harmonies dress themselves for eye and ear
with a blessedness all saints approve.
I shall now impose these buds the doctor universalis
has sent you, while he speaks of God,
the elegant architect, at work on a regal palace
with the "subtle chains" of musical consonance.
You have come from that different cave life,
out of the springs of distemper and possession.
Lying in a crypt, you gather your strangeness,
waiting to bejewel another city with your ecstasy.
Such rose leaves enfold your words that the king,
as he refuses, must bend to define the light
and hear the modulation in his voice that has gone.
True to the night and the cave's rejoicing,
you cover his eyes with flame.
                               I know
you have written this mystery of embodiment
in fire and a virgin birth; when the stone fell
from heaven, it flowered in an almond tree,

and a pine tree covered with violets became
                              a token for your love.
All ways lead down to the politic mother
and the fear of celebration, the cleansing
in a new birth where the mother-bride rises.
Who rises first?
The memory of fire confuses me.
Your tunic rages blue with wrath.
You abandon me
in the ruin of an incomparable house.
Who rises first?
When now this clairvoyant rose rises over stone
in the choir, I can hear the burning,
clearing the path for a red sign and a figure
who will stand suspended
until a red mother claims him on a red shore.

Yemanjá

Dawn on a greener earth shapes the woman,
come, with immaculate beads around her neck,
to secure the figure of my infant step.
I ride, in silence, upon her head from water
to water, through the dance in which you hold her.

Where the air is clear they will do even better by you.
Even so, we changed you when we changed your name,
married you to whiteness in a depth of sky quite out of reach
and gave you thunder, arrows and iron for your sons.
Memory tells us you were made water by insult,
the fortunate flicker of wrath that swept you
out of the market and into healing. Or so
these pots reveal our desire for purity.

I hear a toucan over water call me
to my oldest river, the bird's voice filled
with the clamor of cloth and melon seeds.
Weightless now, I climb down from a green
ledge to declare myself your son again.
Near the clearing, where the deer come to nibble
at a late spring, I have your water-worn stones
bathing in the blood of whatever the land gives.

Compassion wears us down like river-worn stones.
I return to your river body.
Your sixteen cowry shells flare in a darker light.
At the river's edge, a young woman bends to bathe

the bite of your porridge from her mouth.
Even in the twilight, I can see her eyes blaze
with the pleasure of having known love alone.

Zapata and the Egúngún Mask

En agua divina en hoguera nací: soy mexicano.
Facing east, I learn to betray myself.
Ochre clouds on the sky's vault
lift cactus from its chalk brown death.
These facts are not actual,
only an uncovered city,
a shawled and surly Huichol saint,
        out of time,
        out of place,
fangled in plaster.
You must learn blood's ascendance,
the high air it will ride
until it comes to rest
        in another heart.
That heart is yours.
That step into the red flower of winter
begins your first abandonment.

Stars do not circle the earth.
Earth rides its galactic horse
        from moment to moment.
So we must sight through a wooden cross
to fix our own movement;
so we must be fixed in stone
to measure the flight of the cross.

In the Villa Rica de la Vera Cruz,
I wait to receive you.

Cuirass and cross claim you,
proclaim the boat valley heart you bring me.
I am prepared to assume
your solitary gabbling with God
and a night's destruction of certainty.
You belong to a loneliness
no one here will defend.

My solitude is a provocation,
a bell struck once at dawn,
memory of a baby's coffin
       being carried
on a boy's head,
brown women in black, brown men
in white manta and red scarves.
The red consoles me still.
The red button of a cardinal's cap
installs me over my own bones in Cholula;
our Lady staunches my Aztec fire
and removes me from the red earth
       I have given you.

Turn again.
       Open.
To arrive, you must go
    through my green gate
and trust your exile
       to my strangeness.
Only I cry for your entrance.
I have stood four hundred years,
waiting for your return.
Now, babe of slaves,
my Yoruba shuffle and song
embraces your docking
     and the red lurch
of the flag that parts you.

I lie on this coffee coast,
    cut myself
    from myself,
no more than a figure in a graveyard chant,
a moment's pause in the spirit's bleeding.

Call me the clear one,
if you can,
the one buffered by guns, strong horses
and men who have a need
to burden their sandals with strange dust.
Clearly, we will become one,
under the aegis of desire.
Such clarity is a way of building
five suns on a rock,
a prefiguration of the royal dead.
It is a way of seeing
the blue etched in water,
the light of angels.

An angel wrath has burned my prophecies.
Still I know
    my sustenance
    will be
    war
drink   eat   shit   sleep
walk and will
prick and soothe   war.
Book it and be damned.
There you have the record of a love gone clay.

Out of the many pains left
to my care
    and the sight
of an Indian hope scattered,
year by year, in their own bones,

high on the spiny mountains,
I have called an end to the brown
death which invests me,
I have spoken in such a voice
                to Christ.
So did the father speak,
until he ran upon a friend in Guadalajara.
We have his head in a cage at Guanajuato
—a church jewel being tempered and refined
by the disdain of creole bitches in black.
Why should I be more attentive in this skull cave
than I am when I am caught,
confused, and full of corridos and chile,
on the Hill of Bells?
                Your eyes engender
a barbarian shame in me.
                I continue,
where strangeness is a customs broker,
to rehearse my crucifixion
        in your cloth,
                at your gate.

Guacamaya has feathered your fear in song:
        Entre cascabeles derrota gente
        el mexicano chichimeca:
        viene a tenderse niebla de escudos.

The prissiness of a "court clerk."

"But more important than these desires of yours
are those of the Mexican people for whom the prestigious
and victorious sword of General Villa is indispensable."

The body remains hard to define.
Numb it with virtues
        or number it with days,
                it escapes.

Sunday.
I have been trying to measure the pain
of a red cathedral, crowned with a red flag.
Clearly, the clock will not strike today.
The valley will raise its red head
to protest the sabbath's umbilical resonance.
I am the *iztli* above my bed,
a smoking mirror over my divided body.
Feather balls adorn the shin bone
and its eyes of light.
                        Light,
worn on these cobblestones,
is your most careful dispossession.
Sunday tells us that this your twilight day
must round to its end
      in the same square,
under the black frill and sanity
of the same dance.
                      Light,
worn in the sober cassocks
of sweet breads and chocolate,
is the bullroarer, stringing your
unfinished soul in the wind.
Sunday. A Michoacana missal,
frothy with old blood and springdrawn desires.
How many years I have sat
in this city's silence, bolstered
by the anticipation of bells and God's
promise to abscond with my suffering.

We begin
the sixteenth discourse on red:
      red patch
      red datum
      red thing in the eye
apricot red of an April sunset in Oaxaca
bullish black red of blood sausage in Xalapa

    manicured pink rose red
              of unwashed mountain hands
blank red of the matador's cape
whiskey brown red of the offended eye
scarlet red sputum of Patzcuaro
pinched bluepurple red of the mother
              dying in labor on her straw mat
canyon red of your skin when it is honest
vermilion tongue in your devil mask

Your face is as scarred as this my face,
baby fat gone under the cut of familiar
                        necessities.
Night in Xochimilco is a disguise.
You come away from the cozy woodfires,
disguised in your short black jacket,
lavender shirt, sharptoed Spanish boots
and silver brimmed hat.
I wear dung brown and my plain heart,
better to display the initiate's scallops
                on my face.
I know no one will unmask
the night you left in Xochimilco,
no one will guess that these public wounds
I carry mask my boiled desire
              for a locked heart.
    Llegan bajando, llegan bajando,
    sobre las acacias es el sitio en que se tienden.
    Flores busca Moteuczomatzin,
    hoguera busca Nezahualcoyotzin.
    Van en busca del cerco del agua, se agitan.
Now that we have raised this flag of night between us,
we can offer these others no more than a curse
                      and a decent burial.
Even these things will be attuned to the mask,
and the iron earth's resistance to graves,

the cypress trees falling in Chapultepec,
the water-voiced ululations of a spirit
who has emptied us of love.
Descendent certainties sustain us.
It is time to be fulfilled.
It is time to return.
I should have a caracol to contain me
when we meet. I should have
a handful of shells for the passage we share.
Why do I, with only a plain heart
and the memory of a prophet's vagaries
to protect me,
    advance and return,
    advance and return?
Why do I return?

Monday.
A Sunday plaza taste lingers on my tongue.
I go down every boulevard and avenue.
Turn and turn.
Obregón,
  Madero,
Juárez,
  Pino Suárez,
    Carrillo Puerto,
      Hidalgo.
In every city,
the same blood beacons shine.
I am bilious with marigolds and lilies.
But this is home.
My bus flagellates Hidalgo's jacaranda.
I travel behind a blue mirror held
against the sun's force,
the dark glass of the jackal's trace.
I dolly upstream with my presbyter.
Monday, going up,

brings the wash of bougainvillea
and the virgin's blue ribbons on iron gates
                    and houses.
Monday parades the virgin, crowned with cactus,
in a blue, engineless Cadillac.
My cristero back pulls the rope
from Zapopan to Tlaquepaque.
I see now
that rubies of perspiration crown my head,
my spinning knees cut a rose path
                    down a rose aisle
toward blue light and shawled wood.
This tide pull of the spirit out of time
inflames the body. One of us must nurture
the rose cut retablos in your eyes.
I have asked the lady to grant me power
to divest you of your corn and flowers,
to cut you out of this river's chocolate soil.
One of us must inhabit the cities'
                    clean saints names.
One of us must acknowledge Monday's power
                    to veil your civil dawn.

This is the history of the Paschal kiss.
Pascual, deep in his own injuries,
always stutters about my left shoulder,
happy as always to repeat the deathless fee
her services require. Guadalupe calls me
his President and Father. Rodolfo eases me
into my Tlaxcalantongo palace.
I know I shall be drawn, quartered
and canonized in a tent,
on a night when the pine needle rain
disguises the friendly voice.
                    Red Christ,
another red night accuses me of your faith.

What I would give for the sunrise
treeing of that "accursed trinity."
I hear that the ruby centaur of the north
begs not to be accused of this wreckage.
What does he know of history
and a mother fondling her sons' failures?
    ¡Nadie tiene casa en la tierra!
So I wrapped those two in prison clothes
and dumped them in a shallow grave.
    I have never been myself.
I give you the earth's free face,
the double holy weight of your sovereign body.
You will learn my secular signs,
and book yourself equal and secure to me.
Still, I will pursue you,
and goad you to curse me,
pursue you until your land, become mine,
                      enslaves you.
I will assume all amethyst water you possess,
the pine and cypress, the silver gouged out
and shaken loose in the best homes;
I will embrace and share the fruit
your plow strokes from its cover.
I am the father you long for.
I have learned to speak in an unfamiliar,
oracular voice, and to wait for your fear
           to make you love me.

Tuesday
opens on water
and the Roman goddess
stuck in her stone boat
on the Paseo.
What time the morning gives
for trading secrets and gold
grows short.

Tuesday is careful to obscure
the lane where Berta has won
her red flag of confirmation.
Busy angel above the traffic
hears a socio's voice at its base.
>   It is given to us, friend,
>   to protect what others do not see.
>   You laugh when an Indian rides
>   his barefoot pride
>   down a street
>   that has heard the jingle
>   of prince feet.
>   I have often asked God
>   his meaning
>   and urged a gentleman's
>   understanding upon him.
>   I conjure cloth; he delivers men.
>   My offer was as generous
>   as the times allow—
>   sixty percent of cost for the first
>   measure, forty percent thereafter
>   (the buyer, of course, absorbs
>   any cost overruns).
>   Friend, what is the business
>   of God, if not our protection?
>   What is the meaning of this lady,
>   if not to recall the wolf voice
>   with which we were born?

Tuesday is the ache of Wednesday,
the threshold of desolation.

Wednesday.
Sunset in the great city.
The firefly lamps in Rio Lerma patios flicker and hold.
Cars thread their red lights in the Paseo's cocoon.

After the starfall of a soft rain,
the sky puts on a gray rebozo.
Every morning now, ladies from Texcoco
prepare their rainbow thin rebozos
for the city's desolate call; they walk
barefoot from spiny path to stone,
out of the lightning of old age, death,
babies and a forgiveness that never comes.
They appear, washed of haste, to stand,
doll-eyed and rigid at crossroads, at sunset.
That one you see there, huddled in her
white cotton dress and sieve black shawl,
at least knows a journey's end.
She spreads her burred, brown woolen rug,
dips in her string bag for black silver beads
and the small red eye-of-God,
lays these at the heart of her rug, kneels.
She draws into the wood of her own silence.
The winged woman above her will not kneel,
nor answer, nor acknowledge the unarmed
respect the other gives. She has been called
to adorn only the city's civil claims,
the piped and feathered warriors,
                    buried without a trace.
I extol the Texcoco eyes
that will not be deceived,
the antiphon that answers no call.
I revere the ear attuned to the prayer
Minerva can no longer say.
My Texcoco lady rises from the grave
of mud walls and a rocky tilling land,
to obscure the creole grave in Montparnasse,
with its crystal urn of good Oaxaca dirt.

Yet "in the very hour of their success,"
they "have disagreed,"

"and no man seems to see
or lead the way to peace
     and settled order."

You must prepare for my eruption
and the guarded way I have of guarding you.
 I am that I am
  two steps beyond the northern line.
 I become what I am
  two steps below it.
"Do you speak English?"
  "Sí, American Smelting and Refining y sonofabitch."
   Caught bleeding in a cave,
   I suck my rebel wounds.
   Your horses have passed,
   and passed again.
   You would find it politic,
   señor, to buy a dog
   to snuff my rag feet.
   I will never give in
   to your rose tint piety.
   I will be bundled and fired
   by the Indian in me.
   Our contract was written,
   in burnished figures on parchment,
   at Santa Isabel.
   I will not go back.
   I will not,
   at the hour of my first death,
   stand under a gringo's eyes.
   Now, 'manos, aim . . . fire.

Ask me if I remember the giant saguaro cactus,
the Sangre de Cristo,
sagebrush sitting golden on a coiled brown path,
the cream rose end of a dry day.

Ask me if I remember the hard felt hat
and confusion of names I wore,
out of the Alamo, over the king's mountain,
down to the slave and green coast.
You were waiting for the right mistake
to tap the rich water in my northern wells.
I live with the gestalt of your greed,
a configuration of "natural boundaries" in my bowels.
What is the difference between one Wilson and another?
I try to curry Atlantic favor and trade
my trust in you away. You become
          the captain of my port.
      I have never been myself.
How can I forgive my inability to deceive the east,
my lost faith in the prophecies I engendered?
When there is no more flesh for the thorn,
how can I nurture this yellow rose of love between us?
Night has been our connection,
     a doxy of dovegray weddings,
the slatbed where a lover takes revenge.
I hold my pickaxe self in you,
and hear my heart ask, who will be redeemed,
who will figure the native body
         and the dark home,
fit for our dark light?

      I must become myself.
I must learn to say I forgive myself,
    for my scab eyes and dropped caul,
for the inattentive bliss of bleeding the mother
              who names me,
for the donkey cart of injuries I haul
               from city to city,
for the gaudgiddy cathedral fires I build between us.
Still, I call the resurrection once again:
      Francisco Madero,

      José María Pino Suárez,
      Belisario Domínguez,
      Serapio Rendón,
      Adolfo Bassó.
Out of the rock of betrayal,
I now carve my own forgiveness.
    Will it last?
    Will it be enough?

If the beggar repents,
we must approach the Magdalene in another way.
Zimmerman will minister to him.
We want the Sun to rise in arms throughout the land.
      Deep waters will return us home
        Texas   New Mexico   Arizona
    I will build a nation against old enemies
Offer them the spirit of contention;
it is this they understand.
      Lightning snow of trust broken
      A speck of snuff on holy parchment
      Caged by your closeness again

      I have never forgotten
the red battalions knocked up to defend my dream.
No one works for me now.
I lock their union halls and clap
new codes and customs on their houses.
The little Morelos Indian coins his own silver.
I sack my banks, issue useless paper.
I allow the eagle to fly on his own volition.
Though everyone contributes to my cause,
criollo capers on the earth please me most.
Who is to say what separates a man from public life?
The Centaur must be hooded;
      the little Indian must die.

Thursday.
I have come to the fifth day
in the Long Count of Desolation.
This is the day of the dead,
a night for the stone Christ
and the crossing,
a timeless boiling of nickel candles,
to be lit and caressed by the lake's
lily-infested breath.
One is forever going up the vein
toward a sheathed heart,
or going down,
driven deep beneath dead mines
to arrive in mummied splendor
            with a skull song.
I emerge from water and earth
into the god's promised air,
covering for my black light of promise.
Babalawo has honored me
with my grandfather's shroud.
Tonight,
under the gourds and drums,
I shall kick up the dust of his birth,
walk in his revived flesh,
bang the bell of his buried voice.
I shall return the sugar of his
forest days to this desert.
I am only the promise of a trace
gone home, one that my brothers
refuse, except in mask.
So I mask my cimarron desires
in the red skin of mother patience.
      I disappear.
I appear in black charro trousers
and a white shirt, stoked in blood.

My horse takes my sacked body to Cuautla
—death of a journey displayed,
despedida to the "deep immortal human wish,
the timeless will."

It is time to raise the nation
from the will of its forgetfulness.
It is time to provoke a passion
for what is hidden.
The black liquid of exchange,
swabbed from the bones of the resurrected
forest, is only a mask,
a livid reminder of the failure
to acknowledge my night body,
struggling to enter day.
       Yo me abandono
to the trinity of a double loss
I have yet to realize.

Upon the Cardinal's soul I invoke eternal rest and peace in God's kingdom in the company of our Blessed Mother Mary and all the saints.—

Guadalupe-Tonantzin

Night arrives in an amethyst coach.
The jade river edge takes its capillary way up the bank.
The mountain, dressed in its blue rock, leans, with a lover's
lightness, to embrace a small man's moonlit shadow.
At this hour, the sheep natter at a Spanish day's end,
and the water voice of evening calls the shepherd to his blue wine.
Mother night, such a tolling awakens me, here, to dew's
splendor and the rain, a moon that was once mine.
I keep these secrets in a leather pouch my twin has sent from home.
You bathe me now with your other name.

This is a spring in the dark,
hill blood and blood of a womb
that binds me to my task.
I am Juan,
in the wood of your desire,
clutching at the moon within you,
willing to mount your Sun throne.
Your balm is water in maguey,
a crystal that remains
when I weave your mirror.
I know I am standing
where a nation will rise,
and take its heart back
from the desert where the god lies.
All those who dream of being whole,
all those who would betray the east,
will see your image on my back.

I must break the membrane
of my own betrayal,
         to come forth
         and to return.

        "It follows, then (for I have always loved
the syllogistic style of the logicians) . . . that God
executed his admirable design in this Mexican land,
conquered for such glorious ends, gained in order that a
most divine image might appear there."

The man with the flower in his name sits
spelling the ages, heavy with every knowledge
of the end of things—
a father with a bookish son who soon learns
the trick of escaping the book, to take the exuberant
ride down the sure path of tongues and mitotes.
There is a leaf amiss in the book of hearts
when he tells us the City must be *prepared*.
Beyond the Ganges,
when every ear has heard the saint
and witnessed to his step in stone
in a hidden place,
no one needs to remember
April roses, cypress, or white lilies,
or "a torch whose eternal light
is the splendid North Star of mankind's Hope,"
or see in the watermelon dawn
a wind god or the Morning Star.
We stand above a cloud that links
         a loss and a return
to extract a blue prophecy from a day
turning toward its jade fulfillment.

I am Thomas,
with the smallest vial of holy water

in my right hand, come to cleanse the ground.
Oh, the donkeys in the New World
kick up the dust of old parchment,
trying to find my traces.
I change my name more often than I change my clothes
—Zumé, Viracocha, Bochica, Cuculcan—
and I draw near myself in the wind and the Morning Star.
But who is to say that I have come again
to a home where only the Serpent of Stars can seat me?
Jesuits will surround themselves with virgins
of light, and lakes, and pains, and remedies,
and martyr themselves in their own memorials.
I only hope to be true to crosses that rise,
without explanation, in rain forests,
where the silence veils my altar bell,
and the darkness makes my candle only a dark leaf.

This is the wind of four ways,
the cross on the god's mantle.
And there, in Tamoanchan,
I grow away from my gachupín devotion,
knowing how the warrior
            will go down,
       bathed in rain,
how a water valley will echo my twin voice
and how a desert will spring with blue-tinged bodies.

Tlaxcalan virgin,
Remedios of the Otomí,
I am Juan,
here at the crossroads
of a río oculto,
waiting for the first woman
to be born with our name,
to abolish time.
These others come to me

with their sun and moon tales,
their flowered prophecies,
their spurred horses,
letters from the highest authority,
a book,
with page after page of my absence.
If it is a New World,
why am I driven by the silver
weight of an old language,
why do I dress in the canon garb
                of another life?
I must be taken into a sacred asylum,
where I find the new Esther
to dress me against injury.
Through a high star haze
and designated dreams,
I have come to Tepeyac,
to set aside a new paradise,
                sure and protected.

The legend says the dark lady
lay in a cave,
with a small bell and a reliquary,
toting up her Byzantine life.
I say she has arisen
from Byzantium's gold dust
and the saints' negligence
to appear in that other Rome,
a healing water,
                flowing
toward her home on the hill.
So she becomes the history of Spain.
Even now,
the Turk's copper lamp is lit in her nave.
So even we are set apart
and clarified by that light.

But my eagle wings disturb the air,
where I sit on a nopal for my serpent meal,
and an angel rides me
                through the dark.

This is the history of learning
to be properly dressed.
White is the moment
when the wife of the serpent
becomes our mother,
when the mother of the gods
                puts on her anguish,
when I grind my rainbow of chile and corn.
Such purity can still adorn a skirt of stars.
Purity consumes me.
                Lords, let us open the feast.
                I have it that the slave
                has been purified and dressed.
                Tender little ear of corn
                —Xilonen, from now
                until the day of her death.
There is a moment
when the women know the cradle is there,
and the flint glows with its familial
recollection of other lives,
                given to light.
I would be the son in the cradle,
and know my mother as that tender ear of corn.
I would be my own double,
a king who uncovers the familiar
                axis of his life.

Long before this sun became familiar to my skin,
I embraced my own abandonment,
became aware of night's root and branch in my heart.

Long before that other moon had distinguished my saints,
I hung a crescent moon in my creole sky.
        I pretend that we have overcome betrayal
        and that the red lamp of compassion
                guides us.
        I pretend that we are civil and politic
                among ourselves.

Lightning of the North,
Serf of the Nation,
these are only words the others
thrust between us.
You have made me an open heart,
searching for an answer
to the question imposed upon us.
        This oppressed people, so like
        the people of Israel . . .
        weary of suffering . . .
The peasant, having spent his seed
dabbling in cows,
approaches you now with a baggy heart,
a sack in which the nation
pours its petate suffering.
        Juan Diego leads me
        over the tilma terrain
        toward Cholula
                and the desert.
        I hear a raven,
        tilling the desert night
        for Anahuac's voice.
        I had almost given in;
        I had almost learned
        the giddiness of one and one.
        Yet when the desert
        had its claws in Janitzio,

            a skirt of stars fell down,
            spirit rain,
            a wing of the bony cross
            only the mother could ride.
            Even in the light,
            I know myself as dark
            as the bell and the letters
            on the bull that bears me up.
            Given to the dark,
            I will wear a crescent moon
            for my brother's solace.

I recall now the flowering almond tree
and a pine tree covered with violets.
I see a rose leaf unfold under glass.
When I stand in this Chalma silence,
I hear a village voice thunder
like a thorned heart bereft of its cross.
I am learning to prepare a place
where the father will not come,
a house to display a divided heart,
one that fire has washed free of shame.
Having lost her crown of stars,
the woman has taken eagle wings
to fly into the wilderness, to be nourished
for a time, and times, and half a time,
from the face of the serpent.
The father has been taken by those
who would nourish a creole heart.
The basque carriages, riding the streams
in Tlatelolco, stretch their tendrils
                    over an apparition.
Such love is diplomacy's axe,
        the adze of exchange,
a Gunter's chain,
        brick, mortar and cobblestone,

pure water coursing in copper pipes,
a child's book and slate,
a corn cake and chocolate in a green evening,
an eye into time's darkness,
a promise given to "possessors of souls without a passport."

"Doctor,
mañana me la sacas esa muela . . ."
Vulgarity
    and again vulgarity.
These pochos know nothing but filth.
And you,
where are you from?
They all tell you, I'm sure, that they have been
                              to Los Angeles,
that they have cousins in Dallas.
The last jueda was from New York,
and the nail marks are still fresh—
aunque me muera el dolor, indeed.
Their cheap, market blankets are never empty.
My son works along with them.
                My son
works in the middle of the greatest city in the world,
digging for treasures, you know? The life that got lost
when we learned how to weave our Easter suits.
You would think that it would not have taken so long
to realize that something was missing.
Simple that I am,
          even I can see
when a brick is a little to the left,
or there is a chip in the glass.
If water is always running under our feet,
shouldn't we hear its tatarabuela voice?
                When he is home,
my son works like a *negro* (tu m'excuse).
We walk the square together.

I send him back to work with clean, starched pants
and white shirts folded in a handwoven rose colored bag.
Now and then, I send him some local wine,
frijoles, coffee and a few sticks, and a postcard
with everyone's name in his own hand.
I can tell you, in secret, he keeps a gun
                            under his pillow,
and, on the job, a knife in his boot.
But her image is never very far from his heart,
or from his head.
I sit here now with a clear conscience.
It is Easter,
and I am walking the stations of the cross.
I have sat to hear the little birds close the evening
and to watch the sun let itself down
                            into the desert's brown water.
My son,
at this moment,
is touching the Virgin's toes.

                      My provocation now claims me.
                      My casket glides under the rose cream evening
                                  to Guadalupe.
                      Three of my brothers toll areítos and mitotes,
                      and the celestial music which will lull me
                      to sleep in the region of peace.
                      Miguel has taken away their pride,
                              and given me mine.
                      She has appeared,
                      a jade song, set in splendor
                      on my Sun's throne.

Tlazoltéotl

Grainy morning.
Peach sun.
A crow in a cypress tree
        considers rain.
The freights stand mumbling in the coalyard.

Doña Lupe begins her tortilla mass,
the rapid Latin of her hands ceasing only long enough
to admit the griddle's welcoming hiss.
Down the block, where the lilac bush grows,
the old black woman in her print sack
sweeps the gray-yellow patch of sidewalk.

It must have been midnight, last night,
when the wind and the tumbleweeds
were at the height of their sapphic tango
and the moon had fully undressed,
when her husband had slipped out,
going one way with a sack of kittens,
        the other with a sack of coal.
Lupe had turned on her bed
to see the moonlight open a silver path to his shadow.
In her own yard, the drying chiles shuddered slightly.
Cold midnight.
Autumn already promised a long passage through winter.

Lupe remembers the lime green chill of Murallas,
and the way the goats had huddled and died.

It was part of the rosary she would have said
                at Huejuquilla el Alto,
while the men knelt to be prepared for death.
The cross had come into Lupe's name when the earth was born;
she had carried it with a winged heart through dry
and woodless mornings, nourished by sour beans
                      and prickly tortillas.
It was a moment when she would have understood
the desire to clean the view for lilacs on broken stone,
while the peeling house fades from sight.
Lupe knows the black woman sees the desert as a brook of stars.
It is not enough.

Today, the grainy morning peels the peach sun
to reveal the red Aztec knot at its heart.
Black coffee in the clay pot steams with the odor
                      of burnt earth.
How have the mountains here learned to sandal
their brown feet to become so familiar?
Why do their cloud haloes drift with the same rhythm?
                I awake at midnight,
                with the fear that she will awaken
                and see my shame in the croker sack.
                When I was young,
                I sewed such a sack for Sunday dress.
                Sunday. When my husband preferred
                a bottle of cheap Gallo wine
                to the wine of sacrifice.
                I sacrifice him every night
                when he goes searching for our comfort,
                and returns with her Indian eye
                      still on his mind.
                I sweep the dirt I have gathered in my soul
                away from the purple innocence
                      of my lilac bush.

How has the rain-starved voice I left behind
followed me from door to door?

I knew her in a moment,
after the stars had fallen, one by one,
and the garden lifted its plucked head in the wind.
She was dawdling in ditch mud,
                her skirt hitched up about her waist.
I couldn't avoid the fact that she was letting go in the water.
Her eyes had turned blue with peace,
or so it seemed when I looked through the evening's fire red dust.
From that moment on, she held my heart,
and I clicked my rosary for her favor whenever she passed.
Now she hides her magnificence with the arc of her broom
                                                at dawn.
Some morning, I know, there will be a burning
when I step out of my adobe certainty
to invite her soiled virginity to my old table.
She will come, smiling, having forgotten the innocence
                her flowers cannot disguise.

First I should mention that I have during the past four years had a very unhappy time at Harvard; the chief reasons have been (a) personal difficulties within the Observatory, particularly with Dr. Shapley, and usually arising out of personal jealousies because he seemed to like others more than myself. (b) disappointment because I received absolutely no recognition, either official or private, from Harvard University or Radcliffe College; I cannot appear in the catalogues; I do give lectures, but they are not announced in the catalogues, and I am paid for (I believe) as "equipment"; certainly, I have no official position such as instructor. Presumably this is impossible, and so I have always thought it; but I have felt the disappointment nevertheless. (c) I do not seem to myself to be paid very much, quite honestly I think I am worth more than 2300 dollars to the Observatory. (d) In the seven years I have spent at Harvard I have not got to know any University person except through my work (which confines my acquaintance to the Observatory staff and Professor Saunders); whereas the wife of any Harvard man of my status is called upon by the wives of dozens of others.—

The Lake in Central Park

It should have a woman's name,
something to tell us how the green skirt of land
              has bound its hips.
When the day lowers its vermilion tapestry over the west ridge,
the water has the sound of leaves shaken in a sack,
and the child's voice that you have heard below
              sings of the sea.

By slow movements of the earth's crust,
or is it that her hip bones have been shaped
by a fault of engineering?
Some coquetry cycles this blue edge,
a spring ready to come forth to correct
              love's mathematics.

Saturday rises immaculately.
The water's jade edge plays against corn colored
picnic baskets, rose and lemon bottles, red balloons,
dancers in purple tights, a roan mare out of its field.
It is not the moment to think of Bahia
and the gray mother with her water explanation.
Not far from here, the city, a mass of swift water
in its own depression, licks its sores.

Still, I would be eased by reasons.
Sand dunes in drifts.
Lava cuts its own bed at a mountain base.
Blindness enters where the light refuses to go.

In Loch Lomond, the water flowers with algae
and a small life has taken the name of a star.

You will hear my star-slow heart
empty itself with a light-swift pitch
where the water thins to a silence.
And the woman who will not be named
screams in the birth of her fading away.

Loving Master and Mistriss   I take
the Lebbertis of informing you of my present wishes of which
I hope you will not be displeased at nor think that I am not
Satisfied with my Situation of Life—So far from that it
gave me pleasure to say that you Boath have discharge your
duty to me as any Servant have any Right to Expect or wish
for—But old age And infirmity Begains to follow me which
Cause me to think that my Business in Life are nealy to
End—tho I know From my heart that you and Mistress would
never See me suffer as long as my Body Lives and you Live
But I am going down very fast to my grave and if you please
By your Premitions Boath you and Mistres I would go and Live
those other few dais with master Beverly and my Children

                                              From your Servant Phillis

Ann Street

Perhaps the moment of grace hangs over the gate at St. Paul's,
or sits with the dew in the cemetery, at night,
when the jobber's cry down the street ceases.
In that way, some wise woman named you.
But your domain is small—
        a stuffy block with a secondhand bookstore,
        an old tobacco shop, some slate gray buildings
        with undistinguished windows and a hint
        of bankruptcy—
and the signs change at the corner,
        where your own life ends.
I need to think that the holy woman, who called you Ann,
knew that secret and how to clothe it for a city
        hurrying into the deep forest of old age.

There *is* a certain Slant of light
that you see on winter afternoons on Convent.
A Federalist house still flowers there,
        in the Cathedral silence.
Black Ann held her Seal Despair there,
until her mother's island called her away.
She might have stayed, to greet the oldest
water mother, if she came,
but that one's handmaidens had gone into the air,
rummaging for the reason that a saint's name
should have such a look of Death.

Cornelia Street

You compromise with size when you step around
the corner from Bleecker, or when you come from the opposite end,
taking that little dogleg left just as you pass Sixth Avenue.
A couple of trees cinch the street at the waist.
There is always an Italian dough and chicory air
                                        in its hair.

Cornelia, coming from Cornelius.
Not much manure for berries in that one.

There used to be a café, about here,
where country scribblers shook out their city aches
among the cups.

Cornelia, daughter of Scipio Africanus,
mother of the Gracchi and of Sempronia,
as proud of her family jewels as of letters.
Here she lies, just a heartbeat away
from the tombs of city benches,
where old Sicilians gnash the vowels
of a song she can never learn to sing.

Sister, he was so good that I wanted to turn him over on his flipside and see what they was like.

I wanted to pin his dick to the wall but all I had was a couple of nails.

La calebasse est asociée à la fécondité sur trois plans: cosmique (image du monde), humain (la matrice de la femme) et culturel (la cuisine).

Guadalajara

Village to village
the spirit seeks its house
   —Nochistlán,
     Tonalá,
      Tetlán.
The wind caracols on a bed of stars,
warming itself with the fire that sends
the faithful
     spiraling
         toward that waterless, spiny
moment
   when a river's whisper is enough.
I keep the image of a man walking
in search of a Valley of Stones,
     the mudéjar of this valley,
the Roman aqueduct and foundation,
        the Visigothic spell
pestled by a Spanish horse.
   Godelfare
the Wad-al-hajarah of the Moors
knows the sun here as a bronze cathedral,
the moon as a jade feather crown,
and the whisper of a blue fire dying
raises the sand sound of water again.

These spires above my house are doves,
lifted by grace above the earth's eruption.
Here, we chew the kola nut of lost dreams
and memories of fires we never entered.

It seems now that only the earth moves.
If you tumble from the high air of Tepic,
with its smell of coffee and sunburnt pine,
you fall upon Minerva's fountain
and a stillness that even the father from Dolores
                              couldn't lift.
Cristeros, carrying their sun-drenched blankets
of democratic discontent, may welcome you.
I like to show my sons
    —the ones who dress my walls with earth tones,
    priestly black and the many colors of blood;
    the ones who go searching in angelic prose
    for their fathers, or the stability of faith;
    the ones who understand life's coursing
    in a good name and the well-modulated womb.
I wish you had come in the fall,
when the Virgin takes her great expectations,
through the ribboned streets, from temple to temple,
and returns—only slightly ruffled—
            to the moonlight of Zapopan.

I am a trinity, you see.
Spirits growing out of the fact
that my men shape clay
            as the god shapes spirit.
Yet, in the eucalyptus evening,
light shows me all my failures.
My square is ringed with the names
of those my peace betrayed.
Often, my only song has been
            a denial of prophecies.
And when the night closes
on the redness of my most intense days,
I hear a turtle voice
tolling my sacred impurity.

I should have traveled in the wood smoke
of a burning cross,
or been fettered with birds who would come
to their ends, flinted and bled into earthen bowls.
I should have known the sun in a dawn boat,
with its nets sent deep and filled by simple desire.
I should have heard the crow's song
in my own peasant's pail,
and have eaten the sugared skull
          when the house was done.
I should have been attentive to the moment
when stillness must open another and fiery domain.
I should have given my virginity
to a new hearth, in a new world,
where mercy and rapture rule.

Lisboa

Over the river,
the city appears,
a white lace veil
    on the hills,
bits of color
shining through the threads.
Such gentleness provokes
the granite heat of the mountains
        in the distance.
Come, and you will quickly learn
the advocacy of water,
the way it flows
through every moment
    of the city's life.

Al Oshbūna, Lashbūna,
a happy Julia,
rescued from the sounding
of a blind man's fable.
When the fleet fell upon us,
we were nothing
    but gold, silver,
        cloth, horses and mules,
a stripped body
to be deeded again to a king.
In the Alfama,
a Moorish citadel muses
over a shattered dome,
a memory of ravens
        and a saint's tomb.

I still open my true raven wings
in the saint's yard,
and a ship lurches
from a marble fog,
with news from a new world
   —postcards from Brazil,
   with the sweat of exhilaration
   in a new life still on them,
   the dark severity of this city
      washed from the lines,
   the old language to be achingly
   exhibited in the Thieves' Market—
   —postcards sent dancing
   over the Sahara,
   with the angular heads and deep eyes
   of children who would acknowledge me,
   the bronze tinge of listless mission bells
      and failure, peeling away.

In the gloom of my Roman house,
I sit over vatapá, port
and the image of a cock's
sacrificial blood in Bahia.

I know I am a liberated tree,
a fountain and an obelisk,
set at the head of my whitest avenue.
Though other voices have blessed
my marble and undulating tile,
I have gone through the wine
of silver and gold,
to arrive in the intoxication
of sacred water, kept in the bowl
      of my most secret longing.

Madrid

So the villa, having learned its many skills
through riding the bluish ochre waves of sand and clay,
has fooled us again. The moon is only a moon,
without the olive sheen and horse hoof of Granada.
No ruffled lace guitars clutch at the darkened windows.
The bilious green water marks on old houses
only make you think of the candle wind,
gathering its hammer force season after season,
a tempered master with a gray design.
Even the wall has been undone by sierra loneliness.

Perhaps on some theatrical night,
Lope fell in love with Elena,
and acted out her virtues,
until the father bored him.
That could only end in scandalous verses,
cuffs and a ticket out of Madrid,
a cloaked night at a village gate,
a loping horse and lovers shedding
                        the acacia trees.
Better this picking at the poor brick and earth
than the bed where the mournful knight lies,
                dreaming of dowry
      —some household furniture,
        an orchard, five vines, four beehives,
          forty-five hens, one cock and a crucible—
or the Italian guile and papal star of a duke's daughter.

It is late, and the voices of Tollán swing
on the porch of the Puerta de Alcalá.

Criollos dawdle in the Plaza Mayor,
brushing the white ruff of their provincial injuries.
The Panadería has gone, with its bull blood,
autos-da-fé and saints,
and the mimetic houses sink into shadow.
And yet that dead sun has awakened
the mountain mother in the oval plaza,
and these old women in black manta scudder
over the Manzares bed,
following the lights of Taxco silver, silk,
                Luke's virgin and a good name.

It is late,
Palm Sunday,
on a day when the mask will drop
and a slouch hat and voluminous cloak
will uncover the exiled heart.
It is late,
the May day when the sun's red heart
                returns from its exile,
and the Emperor's horsemen fall and begin
the unraveling of a Morning Star.
It is late,
when the Queen has gone,
in gentleman's attire,
to exhibit her hunger for boar meat
and a Bourbon husband with a taste for peace.
It is late,
when the red flag of the most violent summer
calls an end to the nation's yearning.

It is time
for the jeweled humiliation of the chosen
                to be revealed.

Now when the snow falls on this crucible
of sullen winds and interrupted passions,

there will be the dark bell sound of a mother,
crying the name she can never have,
 or having it, fulfill.

Marietta, 8th March 1795

Sir

I have been so unhappy at Mrs. Woodbridges that I was obliged to leeve thare by the consent of Mrs. Woodbridge who gave up my Indentures and has offen said that had she known I was so sickly and expencieve she would not have brought me to this Country but all this is the least of my trouble and I can truly say sir had I nothing else or no one but myself I am sure I should not make any complaint to you But my Little son Jupiter who is now with Mrs. Woodbridge is my greatest care and from what she says and from the useage he meets with there is so trying to me that I am all most distracted therefore if you will be so kind as to write me how Long Jupiter is to remain with them as she tells me he is to live with her untill he is twenty five years of age this is something that I had no idea of I all ways thought that he was to return with me to new england or at Longest only ten years these are matters I must beg of you sir to let me know as quick as you can make it convenient I hope you will excuse me of troub Ling you wich I think you will do when you think that I am here in A strange country without one Friend to advise me Mrs. Woodbridge setts out for connecticut and I make no doubt but she will apply to buy Jupiter's time which I beg you will be so good as not to sell her I had much reather he wold return and Live with you as she allows all her sons to thump and beat him the same as if he was a Dog   Mrs. Woodbridge may tell you that I have behaved bad but I call on all nabours to know wheather I have not behaved well and wheather I was so much to blame   She has called me A theif and I denie   I have don my duty as well as I could to her and all her family as well as my Strength wold allow of   I have not rouged her nor her family   the nabours advised me to rite you for the childs sake   I went to the Gentlemen of the town for these advise   they told me I could get back without any difficulty   I entend to return remember me to all your family if you please   I thank you for sending me word my dauter was well   this is my hand writing   I remain the greatest humility

       You Humble servant

        Judith Cocks

please [dont?] show this to Mrs. Woodbridge

Naylor's Store, Nov. 16, 1863

My Dear Husband—I received your letter yesterday, and lost no time in asking Mr. Jim if he would sell me, and what he would take for me. He flew at me, and said I would never get free only at the point of the Baynot, and there was no use in my ever speaking to him any more about it. . . . I had good courage all along until now, but now I am almost heartbroken. Answer this letter as soon as possible.

                    I am your affectionate wife,

                            Louisa Alexander

Orchid

Old moneybags: the Creeping Jenny,
the Poppy and Henbane,
the Turk's-cap lily,
the pink rhododendron
do not attend here;
this is the domain of six-headed orchis,
with its textured, flamboyant lip,
turned toward the flower's lower part,
its stamen muffled in its stigmas.

Ah, Marianne,
thou shouldst be with me now.

Only you could understand how
     a barren pistil
could bear life's weight upon it.

Nothing here seems singular,
even as it stretches out of its common shape,
a honeyed entrance.
Shall we call it love's entrance,
when the flower lights itself and invites
the winged heft and sibilant thrusts
              of a bee?
And the bee goes through the ridges,
down to the spur,
to take a pollen-mass upon its back,
and flies, with its love sack
            changing shape,

to another flower?
There lies another womb,
sensitive to this soi-disant love's impress,
shaky with the advent of such a love's
................peculiar design.

It would be better, perhaps,
to lie under the ground,
................root and budlike,
and wait for sun
that the soiled water has filtered,
or sit on a tropical tree
and give no thought to its stingy nature.

But you see that, even here,
love raises its resolved head,
where there is only the borrowed
smell of tomcats,
................and the hope of vanilla
................flowing from a generous cup.

Passionflower

This flower must have known
the salt glint of sand,
the bedouin billow of wind,
the lapis lazuli stars that rise
when the desert's sea voice stops.
Now it sits, singularly crimson,
near the toucan and anaconda.

Such feeling in such a shallow body
needs the wet black bough
that the bluest water has arranged,
                    the gift of stillness
that the red-tailed tropic-bird has captured.

We can imagine the moment
      when the body took wing,
hoping to establish itself in the felt hat
bog and closeness of this sun's domain.

At the moment we hold the body,
the name is clear:
the crown of thorns,
the nails,
the apostolic sepals and petals,
the absence of those
           who would deny or betray.
Your perfume invites us
to the berry in the arillus,

to the succulent, festive taste of home—
        granadilla, curubas,
          water lemon, sweet calabash.

So I would know you as another egg,
come from the shadow of the cross,
with the rose wine of loss still
in charge of your generous body.

Dandelion

When that Aprill . . .
My morning wakes in a yellow head,
and I have grown so hungry for that root
I claw my way past the black rhizome.
I know it would be better to wait
for the silk web and brown glaze of September,
but I already hear the song in the frost,
and see the white juice cradled in the earth.
If I were only hungry for the night and the rose
                    the leaves recall,
I would be given to the lion of a different longing.
But I am a bird with no gift for easy seed, one
already fixed in the bitter root.
Now, when these salad leaves come to rest,
I intoxicate myself with the sound
of a sacrificial wine as it tapers
                down, into the dark.

The most striking natural objects in the world are optical—perfectly definite visible "things" that prove to be intangible, such as rainbows and mirages. Many people, therefore, regard an image or illusion as necessarily something visual. This conceptual limitation has even led some literary critics, who recognize the essential imaginal character of poetry, to suppose that poets must be visual-minded people, and to judge that figures of speech which do not conjure up visual imagery are not truly poetic. F. C. Prescott, with consistency that borders on the heroic, regards "The quality of mercy is not strained" as unpoetic because it suggests nothing visible. But the poetic image is, in fact, not a painter's image at all.

And the triumph of empiricism is jeopardized by the surprising truth that *our sense data are primarily symbols.*

. . . the edifice of human knowledge stands before us, not as a vast collection of sense reports, but as a structure of *facts that are symbols* and *laws that are their meanings*.

The Anatomy of Resonance

> And the bird of the night whirs
> Down, so close that you shield your eyes.
>
> Hölderlin, *Die Kurze* (Brevity)

The Bird

There must be an atmosphere,
or an evergreen,
or the green shading into the red-yellow
               brown of earth, for the eye,
surely,
some choir in which the ornamented arms
might tune themselves
        to the absolute A of air.
Creatures given to this air
shape their own suspension,
        a process of weight,
thrust away from the body's substance,
and the depths of a woman's body,
        of maple and ash,
hold the arc of another substance,
a memory of unrealized absence.
There is a river here,
where the white heron fastens its claws
to the flat blue surface,
as though it stood on a flowing altar
        to call into the dense grove
of arrested light around the water.

Look and you will see the plume of communion,
a possible intention that arises only here.
It seems that the river has been clay
    for feather and bone,
for the elastic tissue of the bird's voice.
And the . . .
words that begin a theology of existence,
a political history of flight,
an interrupted dream of being definite.

Night

Clairvoyant solitude on the obsidian edge of day.
A vermilion moon ignites the limestone
    in a hidden well.
It is time to rewrite the history of darkness
and the way our ballbearing stars slip around
    and away from each other.
In this hemisphere,
the Milky Way is a celestial river,
sister of the wet star that shines
    in the Valley at Cuzco.
In this place,
a llama, standing in star heat,
defines eternity, and a pecked cross
orients the marriage of sun and moon
    along the Street of the Dead.
Here, there is no mystery in light's absence;
there is only a radiant voice, rising
from the regal cloth of a liberating air.

Whirs

The jackal has learned to sing in the ash,
a severe chanty in praise of the cock and the fish,
of the aureole balm of evening.
When the moment arrives for singing,
palm leaves that are heavy with windlessness
                vibrate to a star's breath,
and the ear, attuned to all the harmonies of neglect,
lifts the soteriological wisdom of loss
                from its parish bed.
There is a moment when the boy comes out of the wood,
his feet slippered with a bee sound, his face
turned to the bull roar following his flight.
The boy carries an apple sound in his head,
something to enhance the dissonant eruption
                of his new morning.
Now, mother night has dressed herself
to dance to the dulcimer of his spring.
Father now to the boy,
she will lock his arms, and twirl him,
and fill his body with the deep
and devastating hum of the jackal's song.

Down

Under the rock, in the hollow,
there are stones the color of cats' eyes.
Old women who have seen these eyes
know that the body should be eiderdown
and bathed with the water of holy wells
and mineral springs, a blue water

with just the hint of hardness
        and a slight taste of sulfur.
So the sinistra side of that other body
would drift to the North Sea,
and come adown in its emerald armor,
to be welcomed in a Latin wood,
where a crescent moon peeks over
        the empty seawall.
My dunum and dum boots quiver
on the qui vive,
    anxious
to enlist water again
        to unruffle and fix
the mystery of buried stone.

Close

Time and the deductive season
teach an intimacy, reason
enough to set sail under seal,
a tenaciously secret keel
of abbeys and cathedrals, found
in the strictest boroughs, the round
plot of land dense with unicorns;
as in a soul's tapestry, horns
flagellate the air. Now confined
near an emerald sun, defined
by my spirit's strictest account,
I cling to my dole, and dismount.
I have filled my bowl with the rose
smoke of ecstasy in a close.

Shield

Skewed, perhaps,
the heart's road bends sinister,
not out of skin and hide,
    owing nothing
to the combustible partition
        crowning
those trees
    a doe's leap away.
Maude had it right—
John would be closer to love's blossom.
She had been given nothing,
and had only a desire to see
down the dextrous avenue of self.
Clearly, Maude knew
    who would be impaled,
who would sit on an order's collar,
what weight the father would bear
        against his own kind.
Kindness,
    or call it the valor of salvation,
            roots in a shell,
scaled to catch the rattle of friendship
        and war heat alliance.
We are stretched over the heart's house,
to defend such kindness as remains,
when the sun, strawberry red,
dips itself into the lime green water
        that flows endlessly home.

Eyes

> Augen, weltblind, in Sterbegeklüft . . .
>
> Eyes, worldblind, in the lode-break of dying . . .
>
> Paul Celan, *Schneebett* (Snowbed)

Old light, at this depth, knows
the veil of deception, the water valley
through which it leaps and divides.
So here, as the south wind alerts the body
to the season's change, the scarlet poplar
leaf runs, from point through point,
a topsy-turvy body to be fixed
           in a different mirror.
An eye, such as this, may be worldblind
in the lode-break of dying. An eye, such as this,
may be no more than a peacock's tail,
the infant bud in a cutting, or the different
curve of a voice in the earth.
There is a market town in Suffolk,
where the bones and Roman urns and coins
mark a sacred ground with the sound of vision.
Time must tell us everything about sensation
and the way we have come to terms
           with our failure
to see anything but the blue point of desire
           that leads us home.

Journey to the Place of Ghosts

> Wölbe dich, Welt:
> Wenn die Totenmuschel heranschwimmt,
> will es hier läuten.
>
> Vault over, world:
> when the seashell of death washes up
> there will be a knelling.
>
> Paul Celan, *Stimmen* (Voices)

Death knocks all night at my door.
The soul answers,
and runs from the water in my throat.
Water will sustain me when I climb
                the steep hill
that leads to a now familiar place.
I began, even as a child, to learn water's order,
and, as I grew intact, the feel of its warmth
in a new sponge, of its weight in a virgin towel.
I have earned my wine in another's misery,
when rum bathed a sealed throat
and cast its seal on the ground.
I will be bound, to the one who leads me away,
by the ornaments on my wrists, the gold dust
in my ears, below my eye and tied to my
                loin cloth in a leather pouch.
They dress me now in my best cloth,
and fold my hands, adorned with silk,
                against my left cheek.

Gold lies with me on my left side.
Gold has become the color of distance,
                    and of your sorrow.

Sorrow lies, red clay on my brow.
Red pepper caresses my temples.
I am adorned in the russet-brown message
the soul brings from its coming-to-be.
There is a silken despair in my body
that grief shakes from it,
a cat's voice, controlled by palm-wine
                    and a widow's passion.
It is time to feed the soul
    —a hen, eggs, mashed yams—
and encourage the thirst resting
near the right hand I see before me.
        Always I think of death.
            I cannot eat.
        I walk in sadness, and I die.
Yet life is the invocation sealed in the coffin,
and will walk through our wall,
passing and passing and passing,
            until it is set down,
to be lifted from this body's habitation.
I now assume the widow's pot,
the lamp that will lead me through solitude,
to the edge of my husband's journey.
I hold three stones upon my head,
darkness I will release when I run
from the dead,
with my eyes turned away
            toward another light.

This is the day of rising.
A hut sits in the bush, sheltered by summe,
standing on four forked ends.

We have prepared for the soul's feast
with pestle, mortar, a strainer, three
hearthstones, a new pot and new spoon.
Someone has stripped the hut's body
and dressed it with the edowa.
Now, when the wine speaks
and the fire has lifted its voice,
the dead will be clothed in hair,
           the signs of our grief.
Sun closes down on an intensity of ghosts.
It is time to close the path.
It is time for the snail's pace
of coming again into life,
      with the world swept clean,
      the crying done,
and our ordinary garments decent in the dead one's eyes.

Saltos

What do I know of marriages and prophecy,
awakened by a sun I will never see?
I awake every morning and come here
to sit on our world—the heart
of the strongest tree, seething with night
and blood designs, the feet lit by love's color.
And, as I rest, my heart moves
to the wise music in a turtle shell.
Out there, on the river, at dawn,
the men embrace their nets and begin
again to search for me.
My love is river-worn,
nourished by exaltation and the aged stone
                that perks my hut.
I know I must only dream of the yellow flute
and the day I will bathe my feet in the new dust
of a lover's hut.
              I know that there is power
in this water, greater than the springs of old daughters.
From my seat now,
I see soft white foam edge, crablike,
over the shore,
its darkness overcome by the prayer
I have struggled to say.
I have learned to leap
through dying cypress, clouds, spiny sand
and the wet straw of dead fires,
when the sun, a frayed daisy,
stirred the hummingbird within me.

There is a dance that waits
for the fisher who would know me,
and a moment when dried fruit will speak
                      with the sun's voice.
There is a moment when I will know myself
           balanced on brown-red earth
that still wears the blue veil of an ancient desire.

The Power of Reeds

Learning to speak, after the heart's lost exuberance,
turns the eye toward a lost dominion. Now these
water loving grasses, seaweed natives of sand
sing of old haunts—springs in
          Castalia,
          Tula,
          Ifẹ.
That song has the power to bind us in prophecies,
to invite a pilgrimage from rock to rock,
to retrieve the water syllables of the Queen's true name.
      These are state matters,
an Ethiopian will that contends
      with light's flaring cloth
in a logic that clothes the self with another self.
Married to ourselves,
we take shape in meaning woven into cloth;
we learn the shape of water under our control,
the political substance of speech in cities.
Biñu,
sitting at bush edge,
teaches us how to record feeling
and how to invest a reed with power.
We must consider the reed without its divinity,
an unchanging thing with the power to arise
in fens and marshes and set itself
              against the earth's erosion,
and against the sea which moves with elastic
step to take us back into its arms.

Nidaba lies in the arms of every reed—a lefthand
spin in every soul, a mask with buskin power—
and there rests in her limitless changing
to become old, and venerable, the goddess
with reed wings fanning in sunlight
and the scribe's difficult kiss in praise
                    of her deconstructive eye.
This scribe sits near Helicon,
listening to a high pitched beating reed weave
from sorcery into a Babylonian dance
and the healing radiance of a sickle moon,
tamarisk and a virgin's necklace.
                    Out of Africa,
the song's loom draws the maiden
into a new legend, braced
by the comfortable whine of a cane instrument
and the never-ending Roman walk to Meroë
in search of the spirit's thatching water.
The scribe has written: It would be easy
to wash away our sins against these women,
if the waters were still
            and light were a given.
We are learning to fashion the storm side of ourselves,
to come out of an immobile passion into cunning.
We are learning the ground of exaltation
in a political mother,
the full force of springs lying memory and bush deep,
the bivalved heart of mountains and waters.
This scribe sits in Tula Xicocotitlan,
waiting for the emerald to return to the mother.
Stones have a way of falling,
after the reed's measure,
into the shape of a new spirit,
longing for the bleached steles of a new home,
        the slit tongue
pipe of an old divinity,

                          the loom
with the serpent in its teeth.
All this hardness sings in the reed,
visionary songs of retrieved connections.
The reed voice knows its power to protect
            the moving dominion,
the power of the weeping woman who returns
to speak of exuberance lost in misguided rule.
So the reed will measure uncontrollable forces,
meanings which have disappeared,
and give its light to that moment
when the heart can speak to
            land, and water,
            steel, stone, wood,
            jewels and cloth,
            cities of glass,
            time's new measure,
            life's contending wills,
all the epiphanies of self that can be bound by love.

Desire's Persistence

> Yo ave del agua floreciente duro en fiesta.
>
> "Deseo de persistencia,"
>
> *Poesía Náhuatl*

1

In the region of rain and cloud,
I live in shade,
under the moss mat of days bruised
        purple with desire.
My dominion is a song in the wide ring of water.
There, I run to and fro,
braiding the logical act
        in the birth of an Ear of Corn,
polychromatic story I will now tell
in the weaving, power's form in motion,
a devotion to the unstressed.
Once, I wreathed around a king,
became a fishing-net, a maze,
        "a deadly wealth of robe."
Mothers who have heard me sing take heart;
I always prick them into power.

2

> Y vengo alzando al viento la roja flor
> de invierno.

> I lift the red flower of winter into
> the wind.
>
> *Poesía Náhuatl*

I

Out of the ninth circle,
a Phoenician boat rocks upward into light
and the warmth of a name—given to heaven—
that arises in the ninth realm.
Earth's realm discloses the Egyptian
on the point of invention,
        deprived of life and death,
heart deep in the soul's hawk,
a thymos shadow knapping the tombed body.
Some one or thing is always heaven bound.
Some flowered log doubles my bones.
The spirit of Toltec turtledoves escapes.
A sharp, metaphorical cry sends me
        into the adorned sepulchre,
and the thing that decays learns
        how to speak its name.

Lift

Down Hidalgo,
past Alvarado and Basurto,
I walk a straight line
to the snailed Paseo Los Berros.
Here, at noon, the sun,
    a silver bead,
veils what the dawn has displayed.

Even so,
    I have taken up the morning's bond again
    —the lake with its pendulum leg
    shining in the distance,
    the boy in white
    hauling his bottle of chalky milk home.
I know I sit in the deep of a city
with its brocade of hills,
where a thin rain is an evening's fire.
I have heard the women sing
near their gas lamps,
when the rose end of day lights a hunger
for the garlanded soups and meat they prepare.
Often, I have taken the high ground
by the pond, over a frog's voice
        dampened by lilies,
and been exalted by the soothsayer
who knows I'm not at home.
I am the arcane body,
raised at the ninth hour,
to be welcomed by the moonlight
        of such spirited air.
I am the Dane of degrees
who realizes how the spirit glows
        even as it descends.

Red

The heart, catalectic though it be, does glow,
responds to every midnight bell within you.
This is a discourse on reading heat,
the flushed char of burned moments one sees
after the sexton's lamp flows
over the body's dark book.

There is suspicion
here that violet
traces of
sacrifice
stand
bare.

Flower

This marble dust recalls that sunset
with the best burgundy, and the way,
after the charm of it, the peacocks
escaped their cages on the green.
I would now embellish the flame
that ornaments you,
even as it once in that moment
                            did.
I carry you blossomed,
cream and salt of a high crown.
You *must* flare,
        stream forth,
blister and scale me,
even as you structure the enveloping kiss,
                sporophore of our highest loss.

Winter

Under the evergreens,
the grouse have gone under the snow.
Women who follow their fall flight
tell us that, if you listen, you can hear

their dove's voices ridge the air,
a singing that follows us to a bourne
 released from its heat sleep.
We have come to an imagined line,
 celestial,
that binds us to the burr of a sheltered thing
and rings us with a fire that will not dance,
 in a horn that will not sound.
We have learned, like these birds,
to publish our decline,
when over knotted apples and straw-crisp leaves,
the slanted sun welcomes us once again
to the arrested music in the earth's divided embrace.

Wind

Through winter,
harmattan blacks the air.
My body fat with oil,
I become another star at noon,
when the vatic insistence
of the dog star's breath clings to me.
Though I am a woman,
I turn south,
toward the fire,
and hear the spirits in the bush.
But this is my conceit:
water will come from the west,
and I will have my trance,
 be reborn,
perhaps in a Mediterranean air,
the Rhone delta's contention
with the eastern side of rain.
In all these disguises,

I follow the aroma of power.
So I am charged in my own field,
to give birth to the solar wind,
particles spiraling around the line
              of my body,
moving toward the disruption,
the moment when the oil of my star at noon
                    is a new dawn.

                              3

I shall go away, I shall disappear,
I shall be stretched on a bed of yellow roses
and the old women will cry for me.
So the Toltecas wrote: their books are finished,
but your heart has become perfect.